DRAWING IS COOL!

Authors
Steve Capsey, Susie Hodge

Artists
Steve Capsey, Lisa Regan, Steve Roberts

Miles
Kelly

CONTENTS

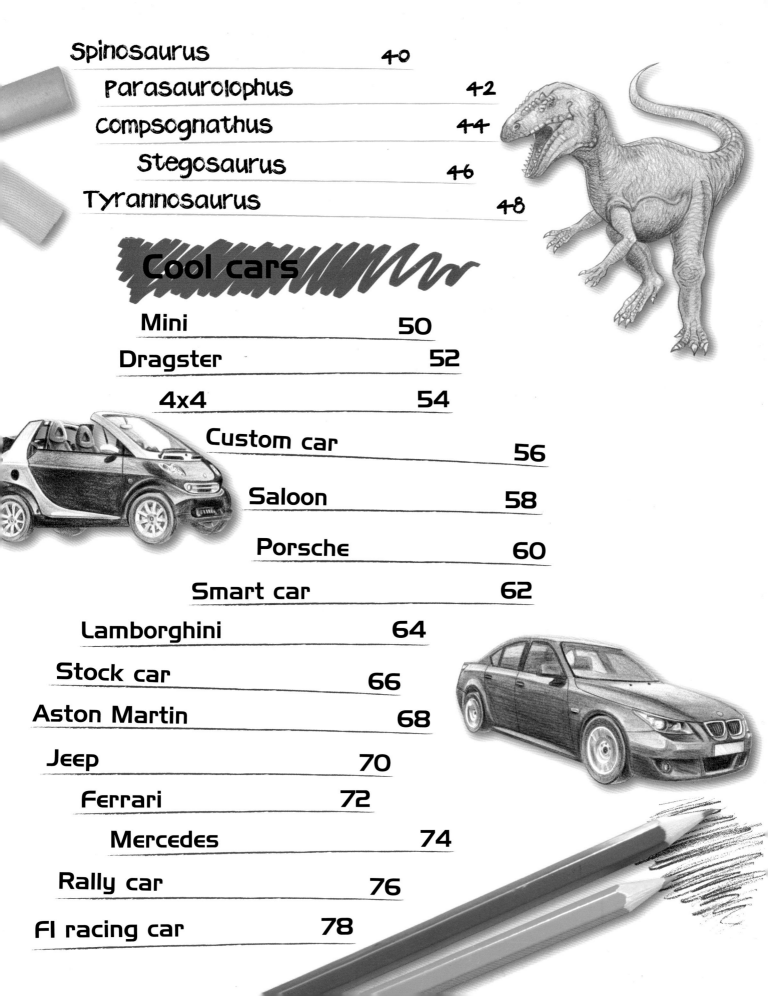

Cool cars

Getting started

All you need to start drawing is a pencil and some paper, but if you collect some other materials as well, you will be able to create even more exciting effects in your drawings.

Pencils

Look for the letter marked on the side. B means a pencil makes soft, smudgy lines. H means it makes fine, harder lines. HB is in between.

Coloured pencils

The simplest way to add colour is with coloured pencils. Some can be blended with water to turn them into watercolours. You can also layer coloured pencils on top of each other to make new colours.

Paper

Collect old paper and use it to practise on, making small sketches. As you get confident in your drawing skills, you can buy art paper for colour sketches and finished pictures. Try drawing on textured paper, such as handmade paper, for a softer effect.

Charcoal and Chalk

Charcoal comes in black, brittle sticks, which can be smudged and blended easily to create shadowy, dramatic pictures. Chalk pastels are good for adding highlights, and are best used on coloured paper.

Felt-tip pens

Pens can be used to add a more cartoon-ish feel to your drawings. You can use them to define outlines and create dramatic patterns and markings.

Crayons

Wax crayons can be used on their own or with other materials to produce lots of interesting results.

Hatching

Draw thicker lines, closer together to create dark tones, and further apart to make light tones.

Crosshatching
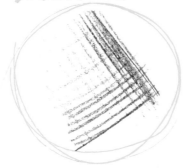

For darker shading, draw hatching lines that cross each other. Closer lines make darker tones.

Stippling

Draw dots close together for dark tones and further apart for lighter tones.

3D shading

Use shading to add tone to your pictures and make them look more 3D. Colour lightly and press harder to get darker shades, or use stippling and hatching to add depth to your colours.

Reference

Work from real life whenever you can. It will also help to collect photos, cut outs from magazines or study other artists' drawings.

Perspective

Objects seem smaller to the viewer the more distant they are. This means that an object in the foreground of a drawing should appear bigger than an object in the background.

Shark

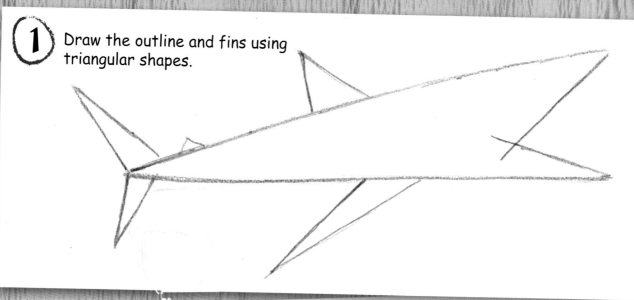

① Draw the outline and fins using triangular shapes.

② Soften your lines, adding shape to the fins.

Add the eye

Draw extra fins

Start to add the detail of the markings on the skin

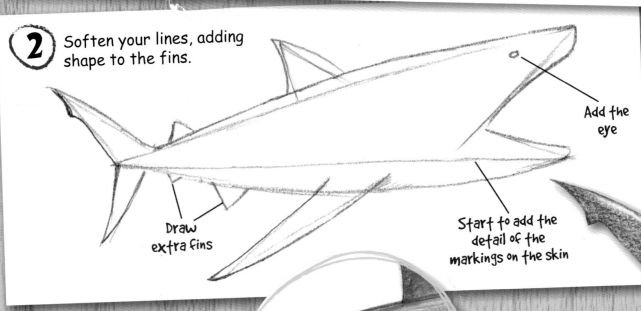

Try colouring your shark with watercolour pencil. Then wet a soft brush and paint over the top. When it's dry use a sharp pencil to add in the outlines.

3 Shade the body and add the gills. Draw the detail inside the mouth.

The underside is pale

4 Sharks have blue-grey backs and fins and pale underbellies. Shape the pale areas by adding areas of pale blue to shadowy places. Make the gums a pale pinky-red.

Crocodile

1 Draw a long oval for the body. Add two overlapping triangles for the head and jaws and two curved lines joining at the tip for a tail.

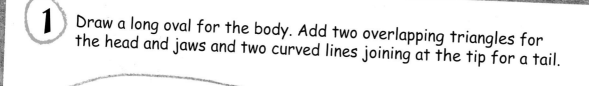

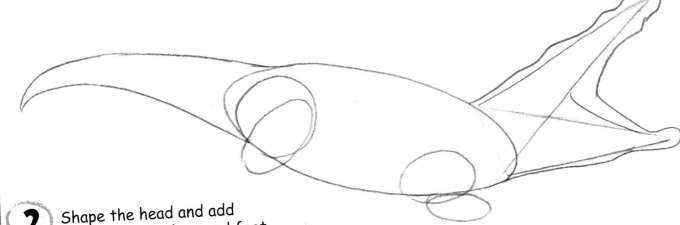

2 Shape the head and add circles for the legs and feet.

3 Add the eye and the bumpy detail of the skin. Shape the head and jaws in more detail.

Shape the front and back legs

The line of the throat is wavy

4 Finish off the legs and claws. Add detail to the head — put the teeth in now — and to the skin. Add shading to the darkest areas.

5 Define the scales with a pencil, then colour using different shades of green and brown. Use soft, circular movements and leave some areas pale to act as highlights.

The raised ridges are black

Bear

1 Draw two circles for the body and add a smaller oval for the head.

Draw straight lines for the legs

2 Shape the head, legs and paws.

Add the ears

The mouth is open

Try drawing your bear on brown paper. The paper becomes the main body colour to which you apply black and white to create shade and light.

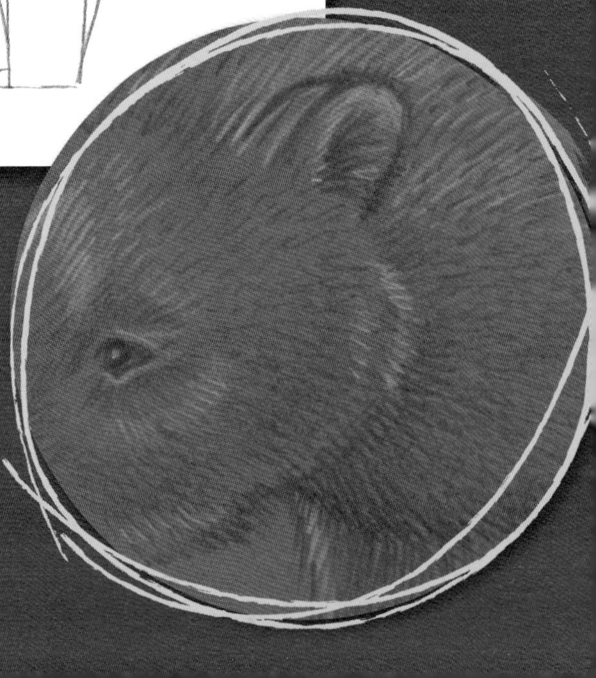

3 Add more detail to the head. Begin to add the fur texture.

This eye is only just visible

Add detail to the paws

4 Shade in the eye and add the claws. Give shape to the body by adding extra detail to the fur.

5 Colour using different shades of brown and black. Don't forget the whiskers.

11

Tarantula

1 Use two ovals for the basic body shape. Add an outer rim to the front oval and mark the position of all eight legs coming off this section.

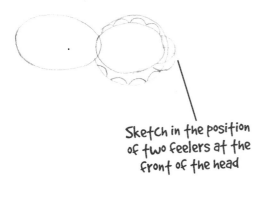

Sketch in the position of two feelers at the front of the head

2 Draw the first sections of each of the eight legs and the two front feelers.

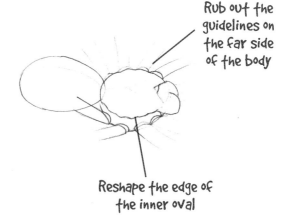

Rub out the guidelines on the far side of the body

Reshape the edge of the inner oval

3 Continue sketching in the legs and feelers, drawing each one in small sections.

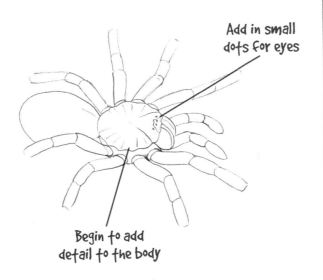

Add in small dots for eyes

Begin to add detail to the body

4 Finish the legs — each is made up of five sections. Add detail to the feelers and shading to the body.

Use small pencil strokes for the hairs and shading

Think of a spider leg like a tube. Gently pencil in your highlight line, then shade lightly above it and darker below it.

5 Colour the body red and black, and the legs black and blue.

Frog

1
Draw a large sloping oval with a narrow tip. Draw a squashed oval near the bottom for the front leg. Shape the back leg.

Add a bump for this eye

only part of the back leg can be seen

This eye is a circle with a curvy line above it

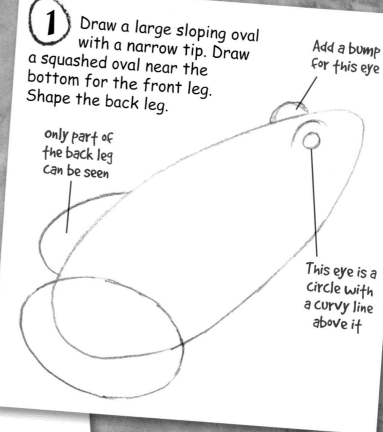

2
Add the front legs and more detail to the nearest back leg. Shape the head and features.

This line adds shape to the body

Add a line for the wide mouth

The back leg forms an 'S' shape

Try working on textured paper to create bumpy skin. Add colour in a circular motion using blunt pencils. Don't press too hard.

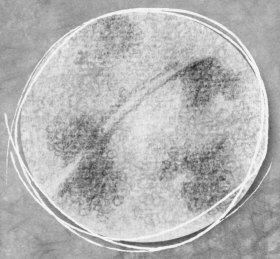

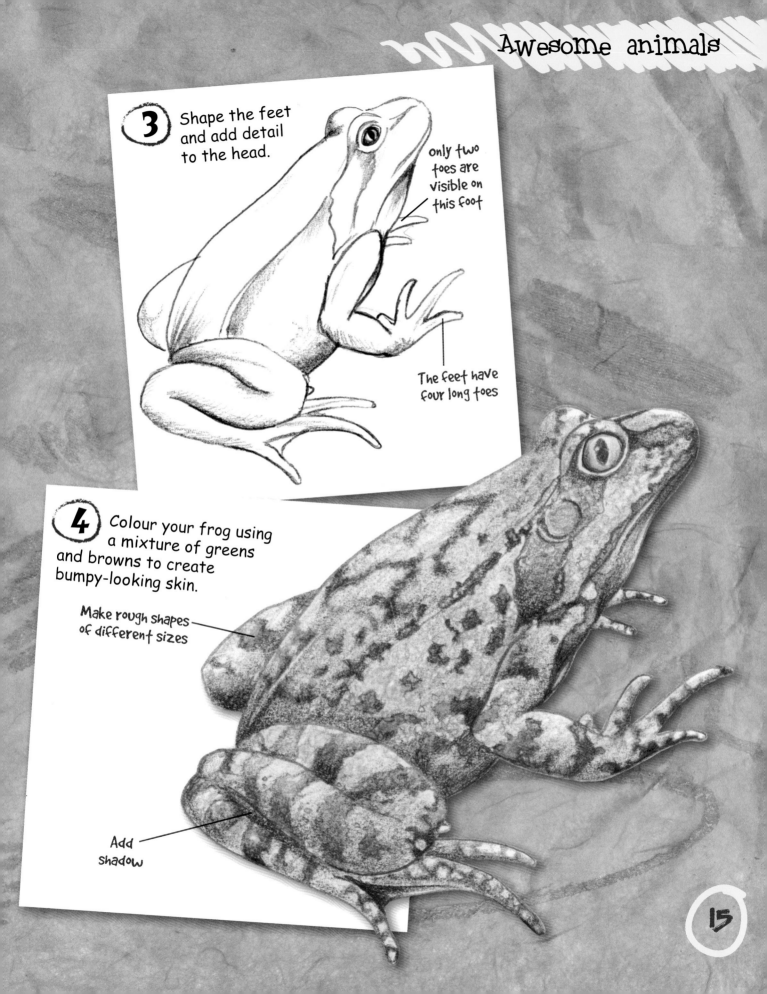

3 Shape the feet and add detail to the head.

only two toes are visible on this foot

The feet have four long toes

4 Colour your frog using a mixture of greens and browns to create bumpy-looking skin.

Make rough shapes of different sizes

Add shadow

Dog

2 Shape the outline of the body.

Add the ears

Make the lines for
the tail wavy

The back leg is bent,
so add a curved line

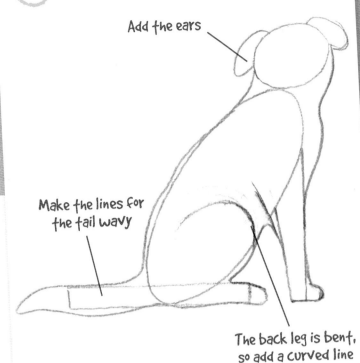

1 Draw a big, narrow oval for the body. Add a small circle for the head and two oblong shapes for the legs and tail.

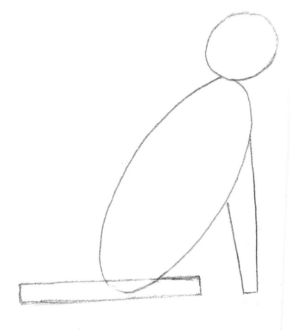

3 Erase the guidelines that you no longer need. Soften the outline to create a furry texture.

Now add the eyes,
nose and mouth

Define the toes

4 Add details to the nose, ears and mouth and continue to shade the fur.

Add markings by shading parts of the head

The tail is extra fluffy

5 Pressing gently, colour your dog using lots of long lines in the direction of the fur. Add shading to the areas you have left pale with regular pencil or a brown shade.

Try working on textured paper. Use a soft pencil and colour with gentle circular movements.

shield bug

1 Draw the basic shape — a combination of squares and triangles.

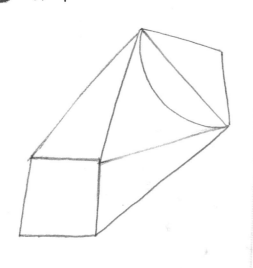

2 Add the head and work over your basic outline to define the body parts.

This hard casing is a curved shape

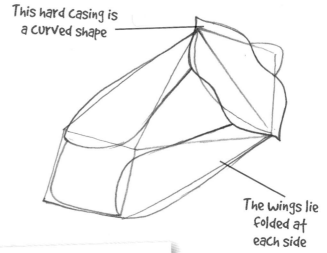

The wings lie folded at each side

3 Roughly sketch in six legs and the antennae. Rub out your guidelines now.

Add the eyes at the sides of the head

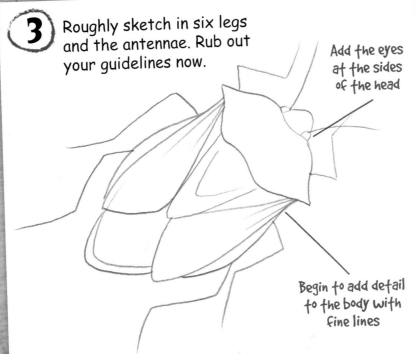

Begin to add detail to the body with fine lines

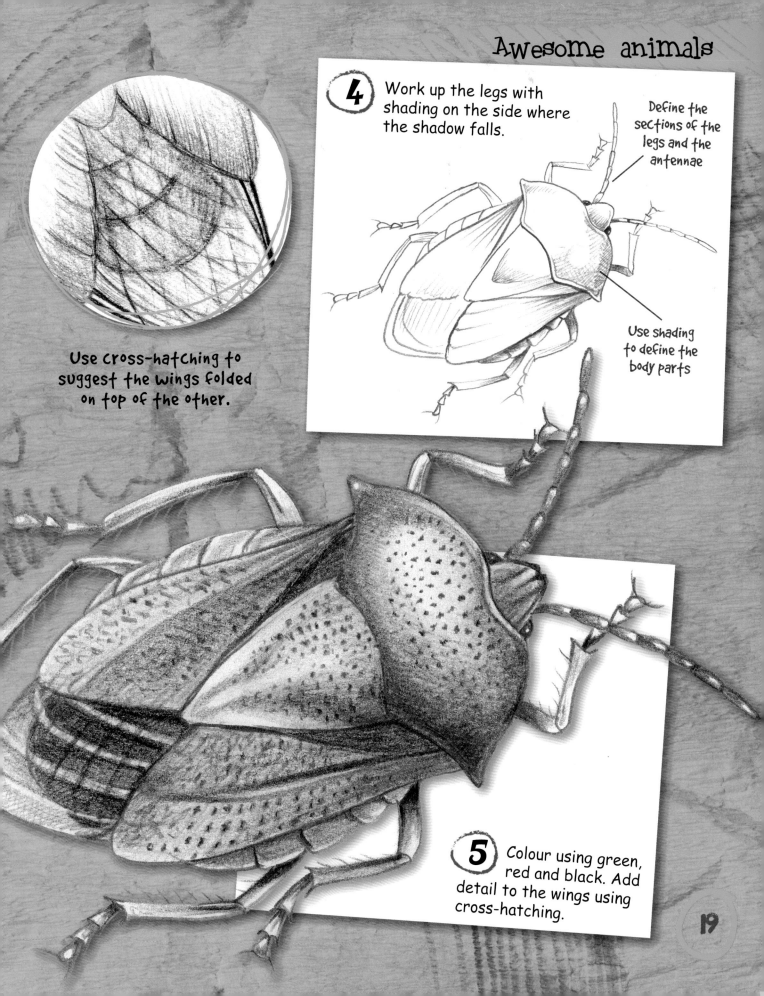

Use cross-hatching to suggest the wings folded on top of the other.

4 Work up the legs with shading on the side where the shadow falls.

Define the sections of the legs and the antennae

Use shading to define the body parts

5 Colour using green, red and black. Add detail to the wings using cross-hatching.

19

Brachiosaurus

1 Draw a large oval body, with four thick legs, a long neck and a small round head.

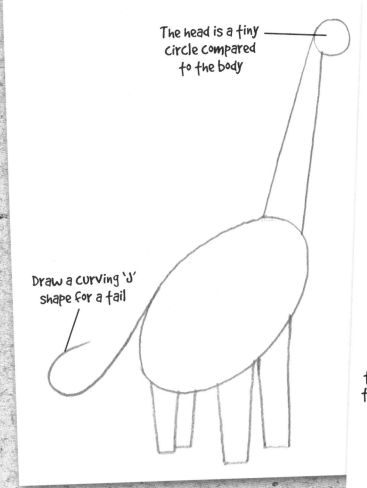

The head is a tiny circle compared to the body

Draw a curving 'J' shape for a tail

2 Shape the legs and neck using curving lines. Add the snout and the eye.

curve the neck

Thicken the tail to fit on the oval body

3 To show tone, lightly hatch little lines where the light does not reach.

Add a crest to the head and draw the open mouth

Don't forget the toenails

4 Add colour using soft blues and greys. Make the skin look textured by drawing in rough horizontal strokes over the base colour.

Shadowy areas are dark, with highlights of reddish-pink

Try working on dark paper, drawing shadows in black and dark purple, and highlights in white and pale blue.

Allosaurus

1 Draw the body and legs as a collection of triangles, and add a curving tail.

The leg behind is smaller than the leg in front

2 Add curves around the outside of your guidelines. The curve at the back of the head is similar to the curve of the back.

Add pointed shapes for the front legs

3 Rub out the guidelines and add details — the claws, mouth, eye and the ridges on top of the snout.

4 Show tone and texture using light pencil marks, leaving the paper white where the light is shining. Draw in the teeth.

5 Colour your drawing using green, then add orange to highlight. Use slightly rough markings on the body to show the scaly texture of the skin.

Try drawing on textured paper. Use blunt pencils to create a base colour. Then use a brown pencil to add circular shapes and squiggly lines on top.

HERRERASAURUS

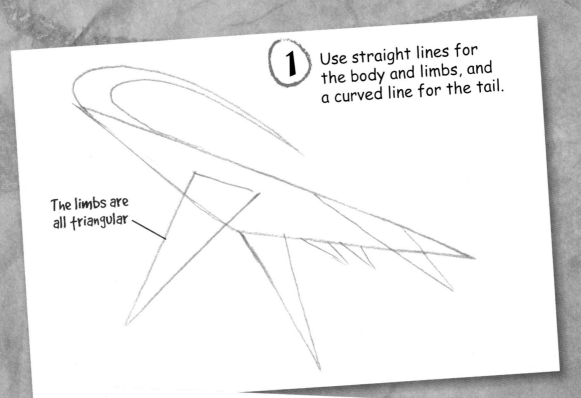

1 Use straight lines for the body and limbs, and a curved line for the tail.

The limbs are all triangular

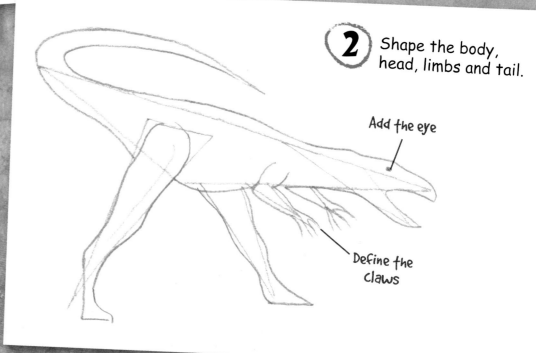

2 Shape the body, head, limbs and tail.

Add the eye

Define the claws

create the look of wrinkled skin by drawing dark lines that fork (split in two) over the base colour.

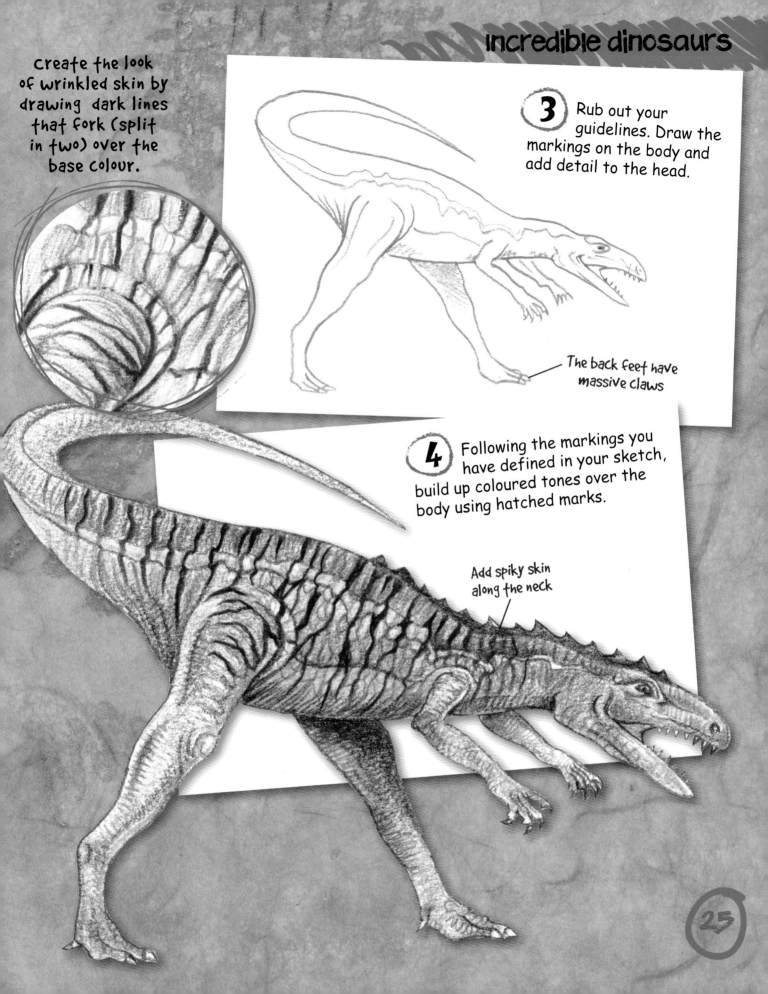

3 Rub out your guidelines. Draw the markings on the body and add detail to the head.

The back feet have massive claws

4 Following the markings you have defined in your sketch, build up coloured tones over the body using hatched marks.

Add spiky skin along the neck

25

ornithomimus

1 Draw a triangle for the body. Add lines for the neck, limbs and tail and draw a small circle for the head.

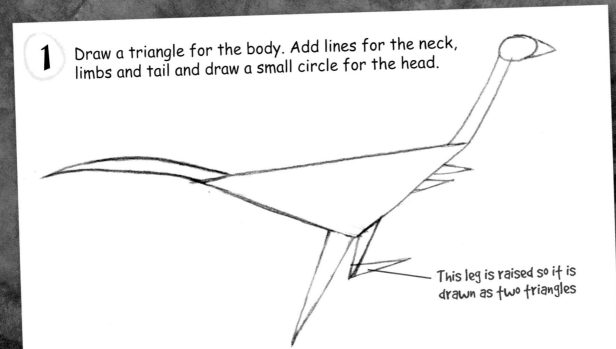

This leg is raised so it is drawn as two triangles

2 Soften the curve of the back and body. Shape the neck, tail and limbs around your guidelines. Draw the eye and beak, and three claws at the end of each limb.

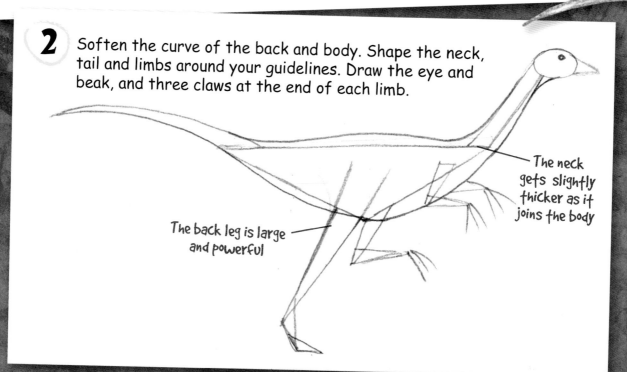

The neck gets slightly thicker as it joins the body

The back leg is large and powerful

3 Show texture by drawing lines to show the muscles on the neck, body and tail. Shade the darker areas and add detail to the features.

Shape the legs

4 Blend colours, working from dark blue on the back to yellow for the belly. Use your pencil to add a few circular scales and spots.

Dilophosaurus

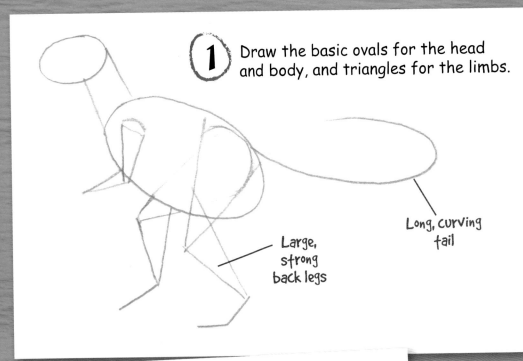

1 Draw the basic ovals for the head and body, and triangles for the limbs.

Long, curving tail

Large, strong back legs

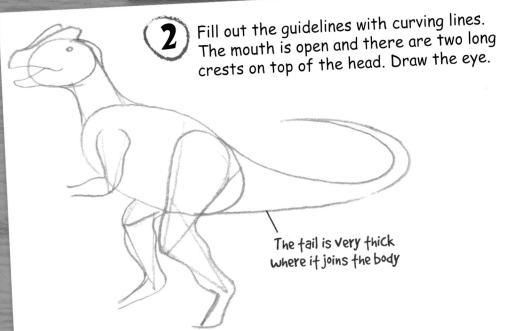

2 Fill out the guidelines with curving lines. The mouth is open and there are two long crests on top of the head. Draw the eye.

The tail is very thick where it joins the body

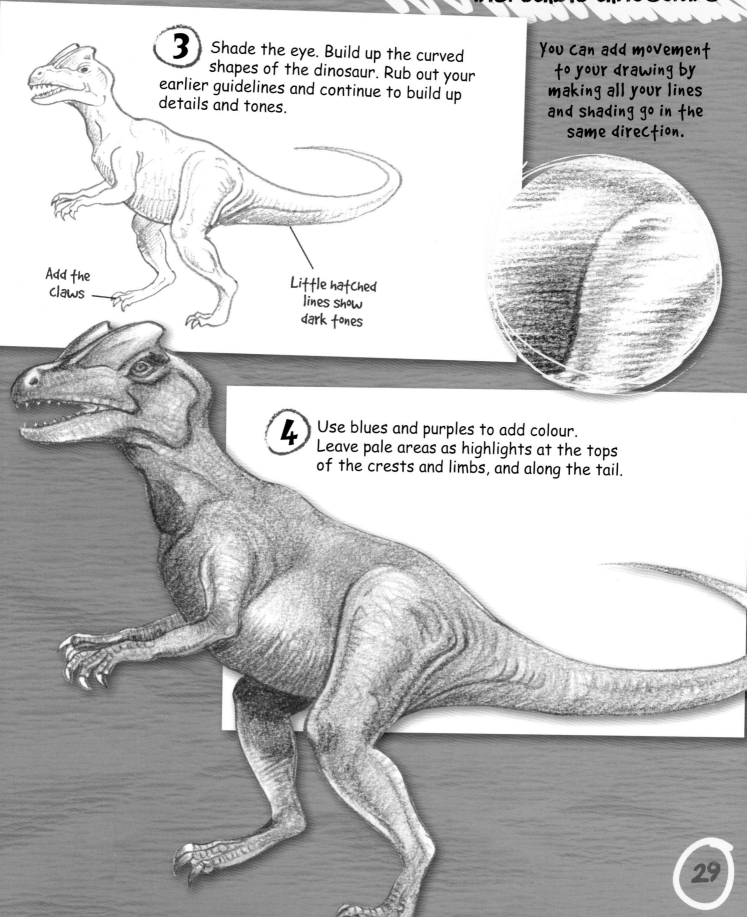

3 Shade the eye. Build up the curved shapes of the dinosaur. Rub out your earlier guidelines and continue to build up details and tones.

You can add movement to your drawing by making all your lines and shading go in the same direction.

Add the claws

Little hatched lines show dark tones

4 Use blues and purples to add colour. Leave pale areas as highlights at the tops of the crests and limbs, and along the tail.

29

Deinonychus

1 Draw an oval for the body and lines for the neck. Add triangles for the limbs and the head.

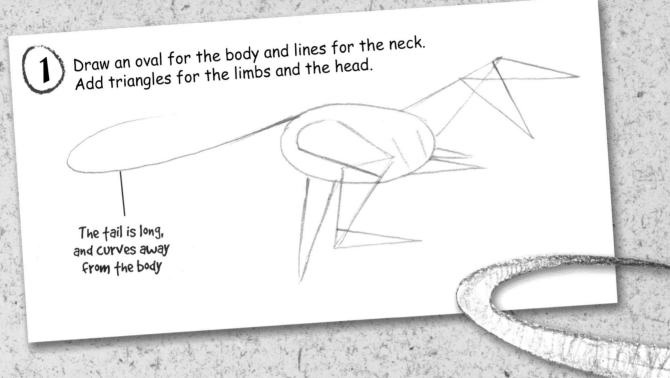

The tail is long, and curves away from the body

2 Shape the muscular curves of the legs, and the head with its powerful jaws.

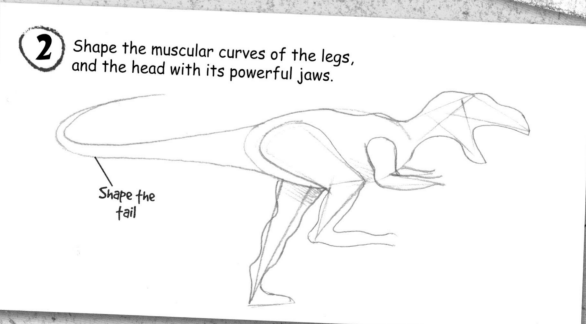

Shape the tail

3 Add claws and sharp teeth and build up dark tones underneath the body and on the back leg.

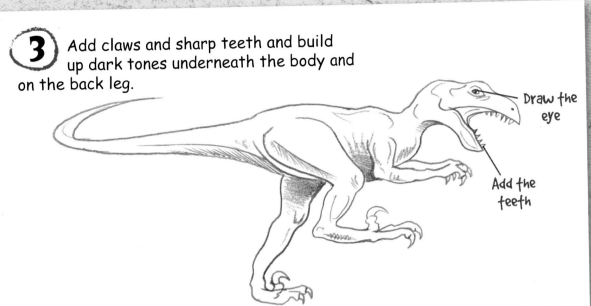

Draw the eye

Add the teeth

4 Use a dark orange as a base colour, making it stronger and brighter on the head. Draw the markings in blue on the back and legs.

Polacanthus

1 Draw an oval with four straight legs at the bottom, and then add a curved tail at the back.

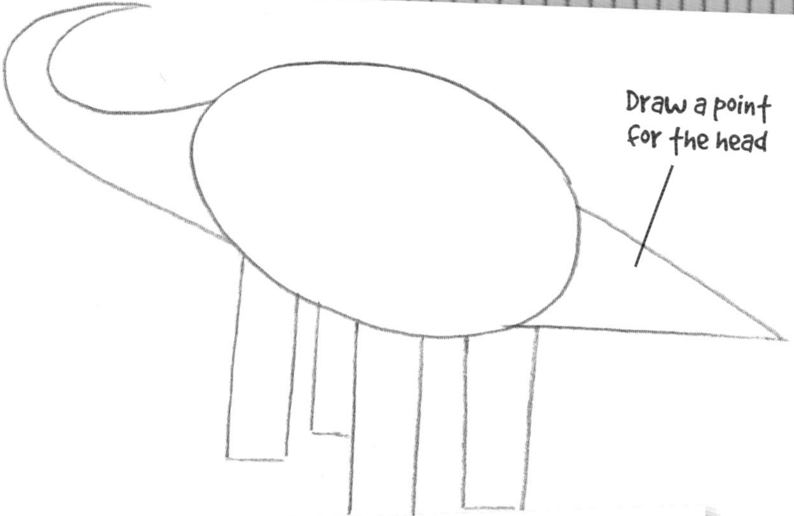

Draw a point for the head

2 Show the shape of the knee joints on the legs and build up the head shape, keeping the neck the same width.

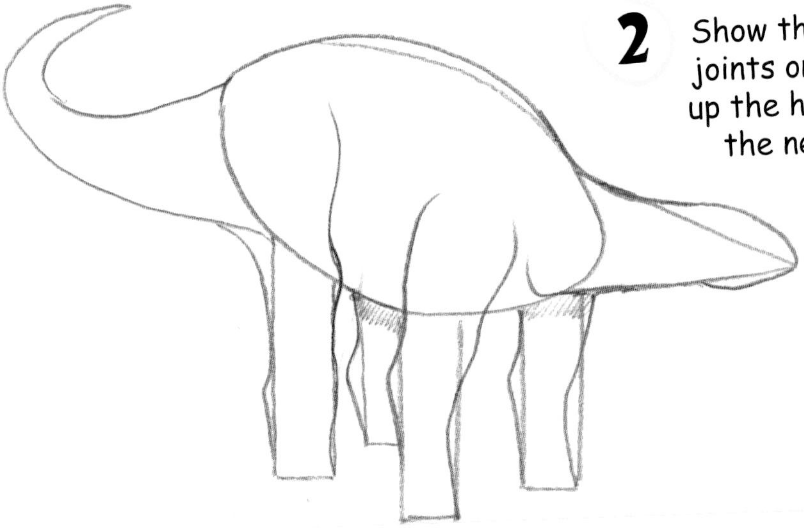

3 Build up the tones with softly hatched lines on the tops of the legs and the underside of the tail. Start to rub out your guidelines.

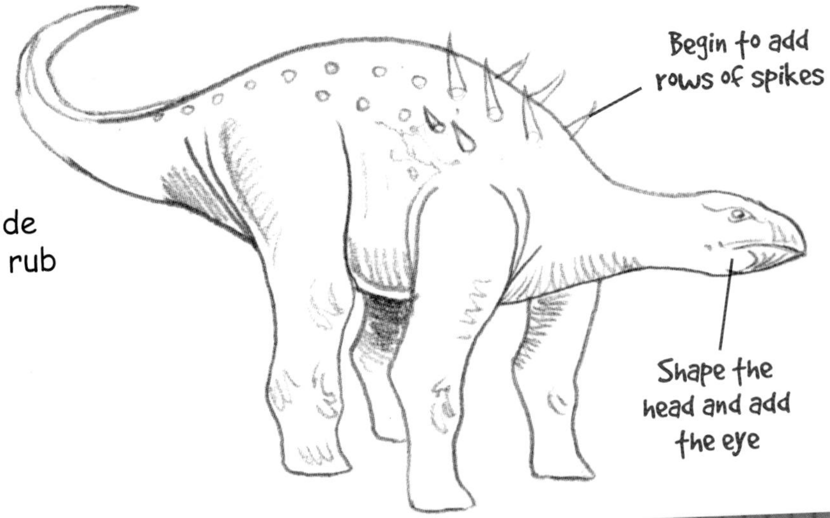

Begin to add rows of spikes

Shape the head and add the eye

4 Continue drawing the rows of spikes to the end of the tail. Add a few circles on the body to show the scaly texture.

Darken the shading on the legs

5 Use a soft brown over the lower half of the body. Without pressing hard, colour the back and the top areas of the head and tail using blue. With the same pencil, define some of the scales, pressing more firmly.

Colour the spikes cream, and add a brown shadow on each one

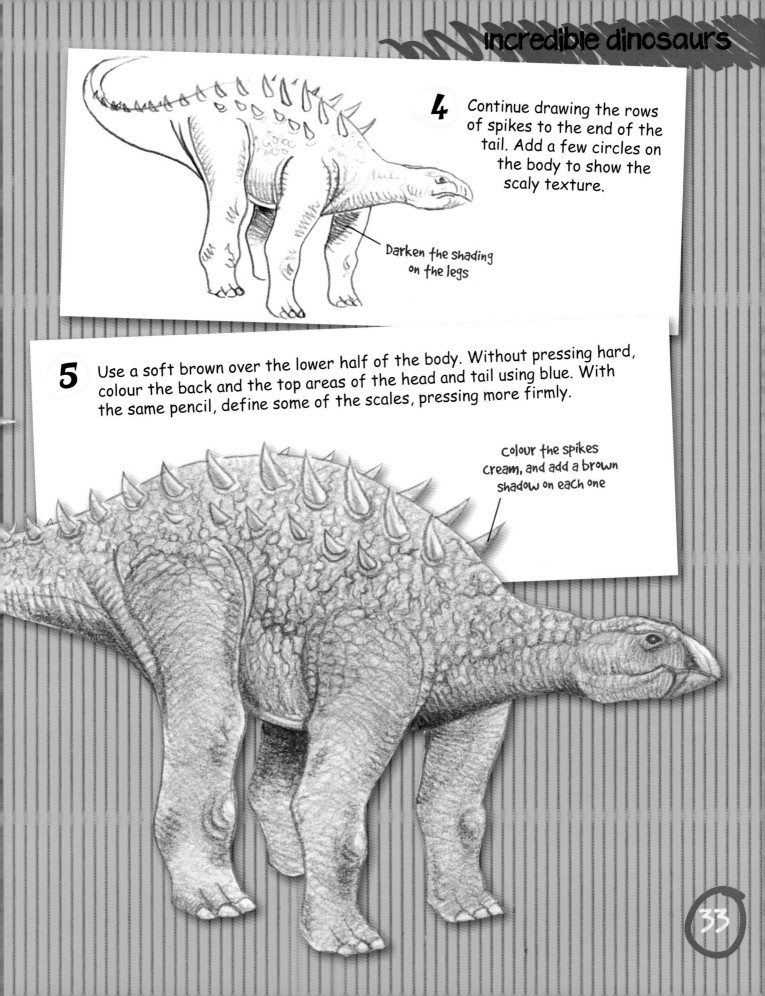

33

Triceratops

1 Draw an oval that ends in a point at one end. Add four legs and a curving tail.

The neck frill starts as a semi-circle

2 Add the horns, and begin to shape the head by drawing the beaklike mouth.

3 Start to shade in the tones and wrinkles under and around the legs. Shape the head and the neck frill.

Draw the eye

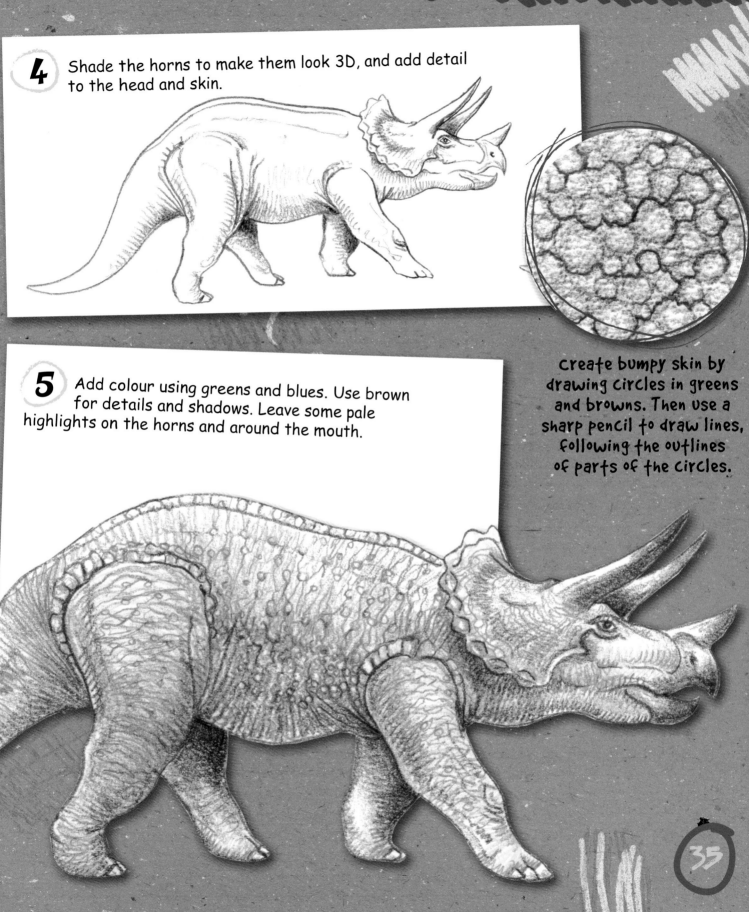

4 Shade the horns to make them look 3D, and add detail to the head and skin.

5 Add colour using greens and blues. Use brown for details and shadows. Leave some pale highlights on the horns and around the mouth.

Create bumpy skin by drawing circles in greens and browns. Then use a sharp pencil to draw lines, following the outlines of parts of the circles.

35

Ankylosaurus

1 Draw a large oval for the body and a circle for the head, with four spikes on it. Add the curved tail and four legs.

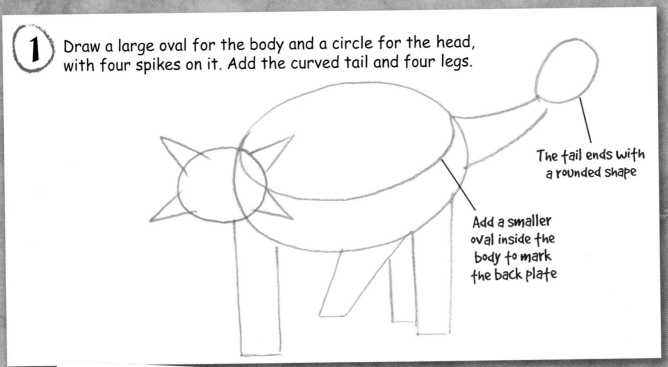

The tail ends with a rounded shape

Add a smaller oval inside the body to mark the back plate

2 Draw curved lines over the back, making them even. Shape the legs.

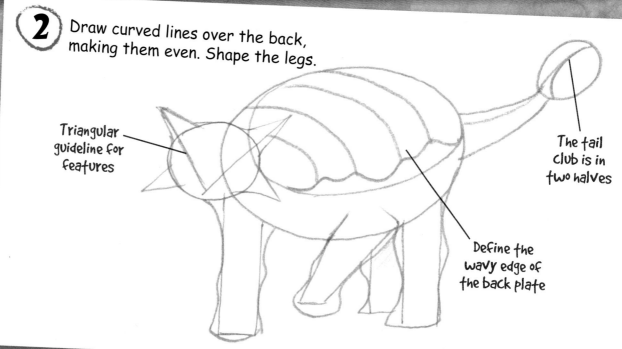

Triangular guideline for features

The tail club is in two halves

Define the wavy edge of the back plate

3 Add rows of spikes on the back plate. Draw the detail on the head and shade the body and legs.

The spikes that are furthest away are smallest

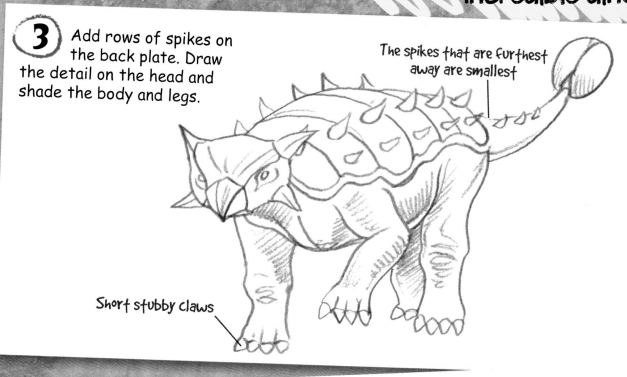

Short stubby claws

4 Make the body orange and the back plate blue. The spikes are bone-coloured with brown shadows.

Colour in small circles, pressing quite hard to create the rough texture

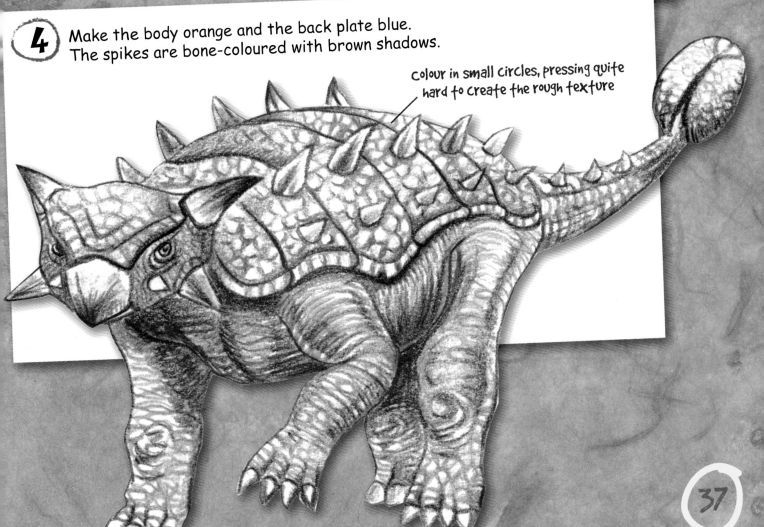

velociraptor

1 Draw a rounded body and a curving tail. Create the head and limbs using triangular shapes.

2 Draw the long, flat snout, pointed toes and curved neck.

Shape the jaws

3 Rub out the guides and add detail and tone with soft lines. Draw the teeth and claws.

Darken features

This line adds perspective to the tail

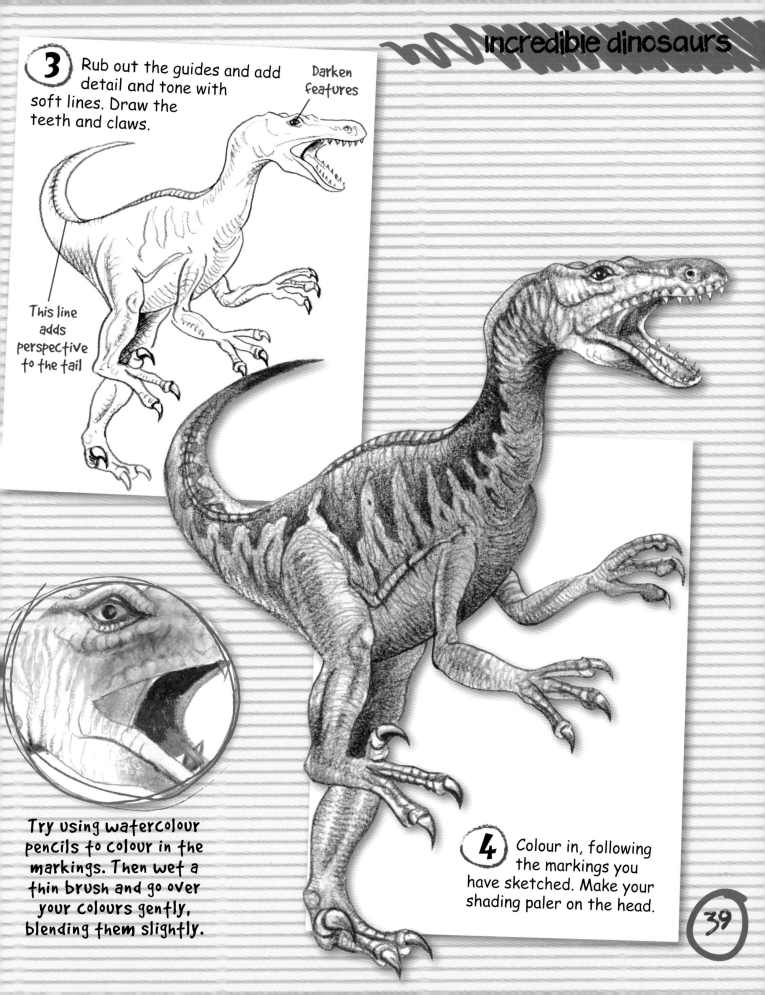

Try using watercolour pencils to colour in the markings. Then wet a thin brush and go over your colours gently, blending them slightly.

4 Colour in, following the markings you have sketched. Make your shading paler on the head.

Spinosaurus

1 Draw a circle. Add the pointed head, tail and limbs.

Scissor-like mouth

2 Shape the neck, and the open-jawed head. Draw the feet and add claws. Mark out the detail on the sail.

The sail has a wavy edge

Add the eye

Shade the back leg

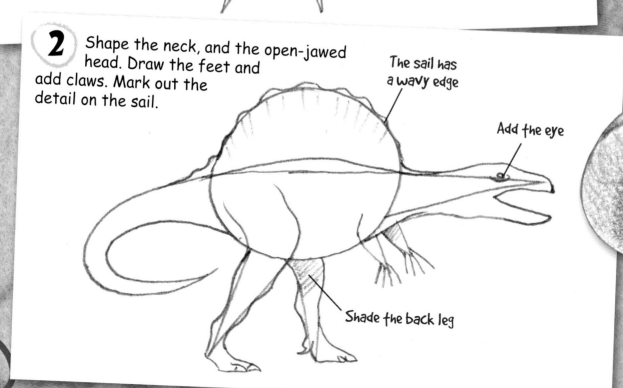

3 Draw the patterned skin using soft pencil marks. Rub out the guidelines and shape the head.

4 Add colour using purple and red, following your markings. Add highlights in pale orange.

parasaurolophus

1 Draw an oval for the body and add legs and a triangular head.

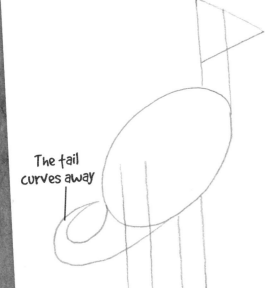

The tail curves away

2 Shape the legs and the pointy head with its long crest.

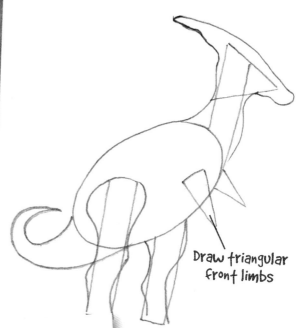

Draw triangular front limbs

3 Add detail to the head and begin to shade in darker areas. Erase your guidelines.

Begin to shape the front limbs

4 Draw the pattern on the skin and add more wrinkles and shading to the underside of the body and neck.

Pointed claws

5 Use orange for the base colour. Over this, draw lines of scribbles in green, red and yellow from the neck down the length of the body.

compsognathus

1 Draw the basic body shapes with eight triangles and add curved lines for the head, neck and tail.

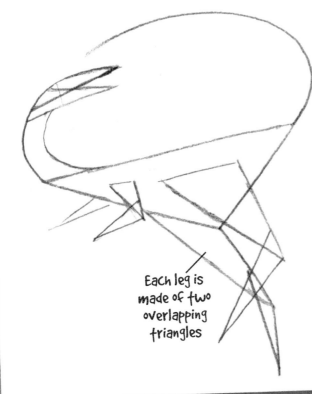

Each leg is made of two overlapping triangles

2 Shape the limbs and add claws. Soften and curve the lines of the body and fill out the tail. Then rub out your guidelines.

The front legs have two claws

The back feet have three toes

3 Add shading with hatched lines. Show feathers by using short lines to blur the outline of the back and head.

Add detail to the head

Shade the back leg

4 Create the look of fur by colouring using lots of short strokes, all going in the same direction.

To achieve a feathery texture draw short, soft pencil lines in different colours all going roughly the same way. Then use a very sharp pencil to add tiny lines to some feathers.

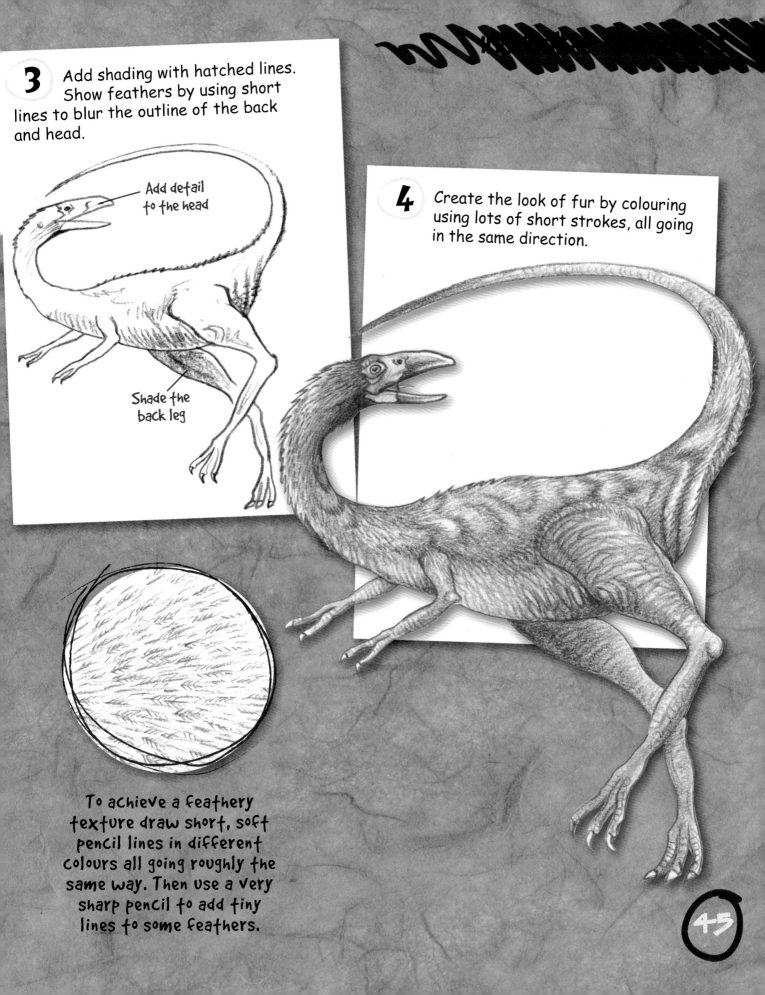

stegosaurus

1 Draw a big, round body, four legs, a tail and long neck. Make sure that the lines for the neck are lower than the tail.

The front legs are much smaller than the back legs

2 Create the back plates as triangles. Shape the head and add detail. Draw the claws.

Lines here show the muscles on the neck

Slender head

3 Shape the plates along the back and tail. Draw four spikes at the end of the tail.

4 Use shading and colour to make the skin look scaly. Use blue and green on the top of the body and yellow and red for the plates and belly. Layer dark blue over green with touches of black in the darkest places.

Try drawing your dinosaur on pale green paper. Then create the look of textured skin by drawing wiggly lines in blue, dark green and orange over the top.

47

Tyrannosaurus

1 Draw the basic body shape as a collection of triangles.

2 Draw around the head and body, softening your straight guidelines. Mark on the claws.

3 Shape the forelimbs. Erase your guidelines and shade the underside of the body.

Add detail to the head

Shape the claws

Try softly shading thick lines that cross each other to create these markings.

4 Add ridges along the back. Build up wrinkles and shade along the tail.

Add the teeth

Leave the teeth white

5 Use a few different greens to create the base colour. Add detail in brown and use red for the mouth.

Mini

1 Draw a body box shape. Then draw a roof box shape with sloping sides on top. Add ellipses for the three wheels that will be visible.

The roof box shape does not reach the back

This wheel is further away, so it looks smaller

These wheels are roughly the same size

Draw two ellipses and join the top and bottom edges

2 Define the shape of the car using straight lines. Rub out the sections of the wheels that are hidden behind the body.

Draw two long shapes for the radiator grills

Add a line to form the roof

A line will divide the windows

Square shapes will help you position the lights

Add inner ellipses to the wheels

3 Smooth the corners of the body with curved lines and start to add extra details.

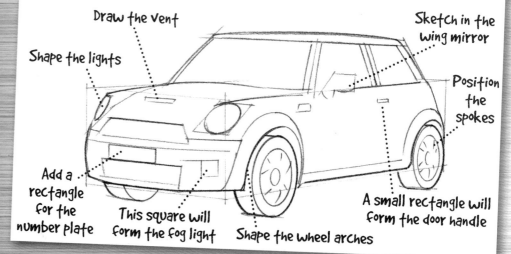

Draw the vent

Sketch in the wing mirror

Shape the lights

Position the spokes

Add a rectangle for the number plate

This square will form the fog light

Shape the wheel arches

A small rectangle will form the door handle

4 Erase the guide shapes. Continue adding detail and shape to the features of the car.

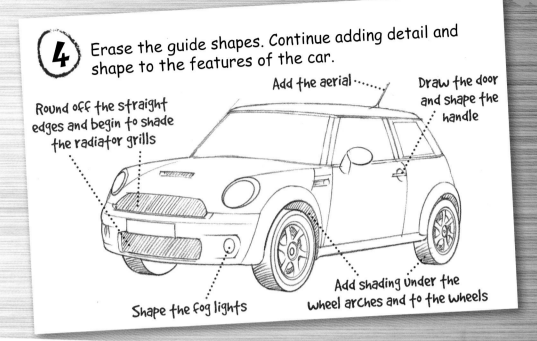

Round off the straight edges and begin to shade the radiator grills

Add the aerial

Draw the door and shape the handle

Shape the fog lights

Add shading under the wheel arches and to the wheels

5 Using smooth movements, shade the body of your car with a blue pencil. You can show reflections in the paintwork by colouring some areas darker than others. Leave some white paper showing through for highlights. Use a black pencil for the wheel arches, tyres and radiator grills.

Use a green pencil to show dark areas of glass

Dragster

1 This car has a slightly different body shape to other cars. Draw a long, thin shape getting narrower towards the front for the body. Then add one small box on top and one behind.

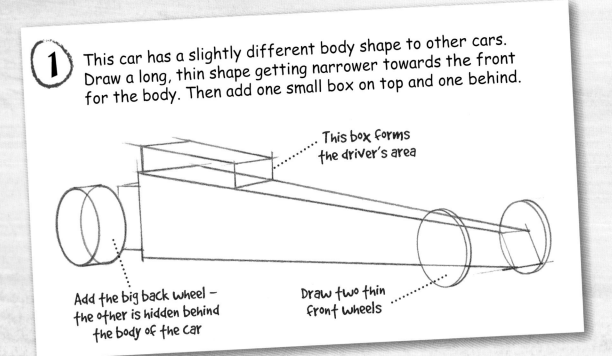

This box forms the driver's area

Add the big back wheel – the other is hidden behind the body of the car

Draw two thin front wheels

2 Draw inner ellipses on the wheels. Start to draw the cage, which protects the driver at the back of the car.

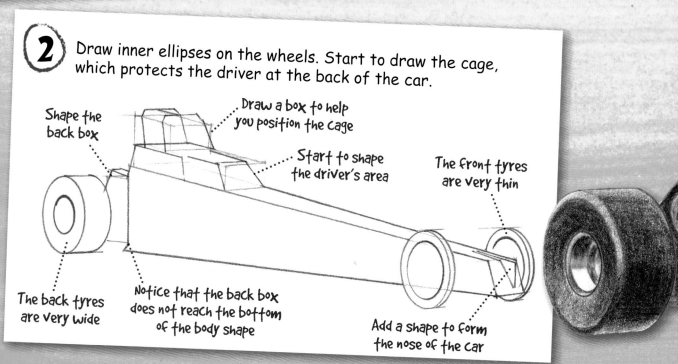

Shape the back box

Draw a box to help you position the cage

Start to shape the driver's area

The front tyres are very thin

The back tyres are very wide

Notice that the back box does not reach the bottom of the body shape

Add a shape to form the nose of the car

3 Add details around the driver area, using curved lines for the windscreen.

Draw another ellipse on the back wheel

Add lines the same distance apart for the bars of the cage

Begin to add detail to the front wheels

4 Erase the guide shapes and add the final details. You can now have fun adding the chequered pattern to the side of the car.

Shade the back of the car

You could create your own unique pattern

Continue adding detail to the front wheels

Add shading to the back wheel

Draw a line to add shape to the body of the car

Shade the tubes half dark and half light to create a metallic effect

5 Build up the black parts of the car slowly to make sure they stay smooth. You can colour the stripes on the car purple for contrast.

4x4

1 Draw a large body box shape for the main part of your car. Add a roof box shape with sloping sides on top.

The topmost part of the roof is barely visible

The car is almost completely side-on, so not much of the front is visible

Add ellipses for the two big wheels that will be visible

2 Make the bonnet slope downwards from the windscreen. Add big bumpers to the front and back of the car.

Add another line to complete the roof

Draw a square shape for the lights

Use short, straight lines to draw the bumpers

Add inner ellipses to the wheels

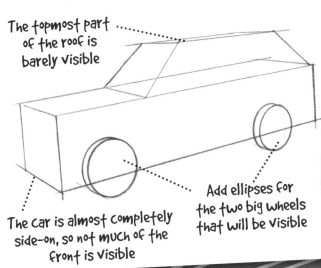

3 Start to add details to the side of the car, such as the wing mirror and door handles. Add the number plate to the front.

Start to draw the radiator grill with straight lines

Add a square for the fog light

Draw the indicator

Show the wheel detail with short lines all pointing to the centre

Add lines to the side

Divide the window areas with straight lines

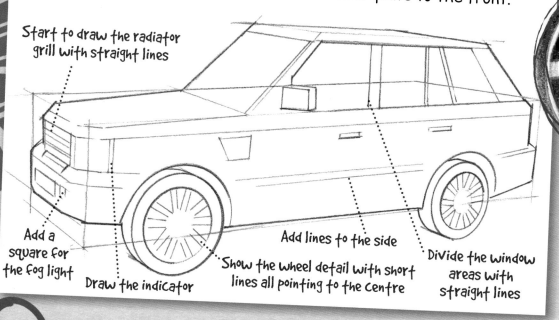

When drawing wheels, the spokes must all be the same size and point towards the centre. If you draw a light circle behind the spokes it will look like the brakes.

4 Rub out the guide shapes. Make all of the corners of the car slightly rounded and continue adding details.

Add the windscreen wipers

There are lots of small circles for the lights

Draw the edges of the doors

Draw indentations behind the door handles

There is a vent on the side of the car

Add shading under the wheel arches

5 The grey paint on the car needs to be very smooth, so take your time and build it up slowly. Colouring the glass half dark and half light will show a reflection. Use an orange pencil to show the indicators.

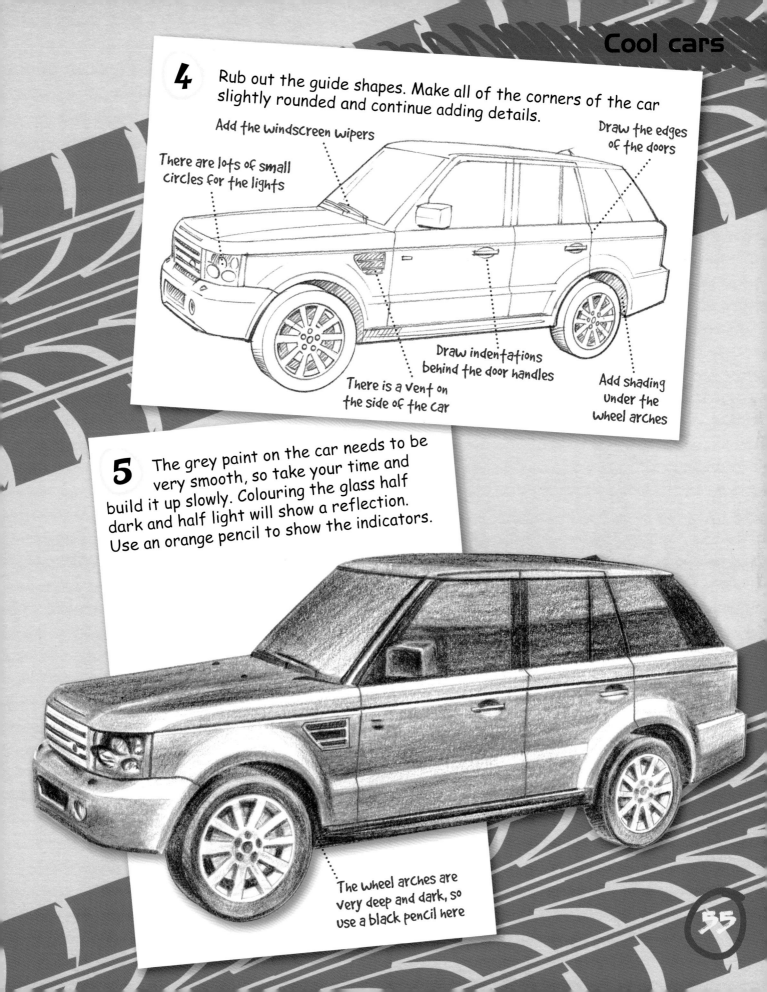

The wheel arches are very deep and dark, so use a black pencil here

Custom car

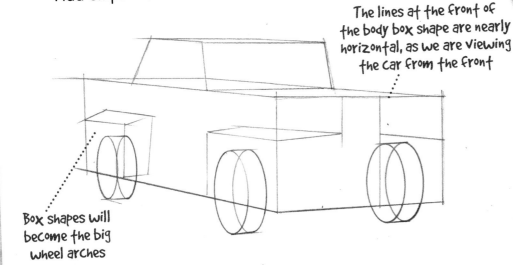

1 Draw a large body box shape for the main part of your car. On top of this draw a roof box shape with sloping sides. Add ellipses for the three wheels that will be visible.

The lines at the front of the body box shape are nearly horizontal, as we are viewing the car from the front

Box shapes will become the big wheel arches

To draw flames, start with a yellow pencil and use a soft orange pencil towards the edges. Adding a shadow behind the flames will make them stand out.

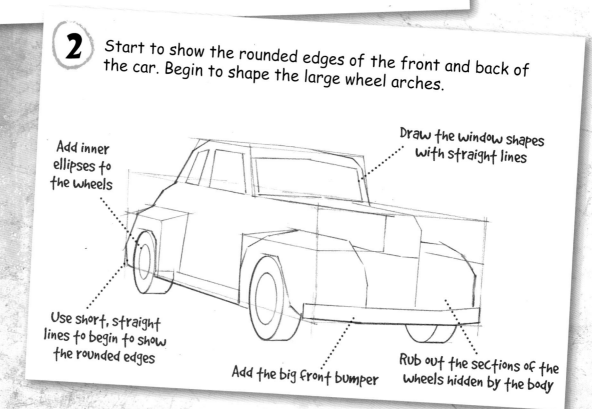

2 Start to show the rounded edges of the front and back of the car. Begin to shape the large wheel arches.

Add inner ellipses to the wheels

Draw the window shapes with straight lines

Use short, straight lines to begin to show the rounded edges

Add the big front bumper

Rub out the sections of the wheels hidden by the body

3 Make all the corners of the car rounded. Using curved lines, add a shape for the large radiator grill to the front, between the lights.

Draw gentle curves over the top of the guidelines to round the wheel arches

Square shapes will help you place the lights

Start to draw spokes in the wheels

4 Erase the guide shapes and draw the final details. You can now add the flame design to the front and sides of the car. Or you could create your own unique pattern.

Draw a small circle for the wing mirror

Use lines to add detail to the radiator grill

Use a ruler to draw this long line of trim in sections

Draw and shade the lights

Soft curves with pointy ends will form the flames

Add shading to the wheels

5 Use lots of reds, oranges and yellows to create the paint design. A hard edge between the flames and the paint will make the flames stand out.

Custom cars have dark glass, so colour it with black and blue pencils

Saloon

Use a blunt pencil and make lots of small, round movements to make glass look smooth. Create the colour with a mixture of blue and green pencils.

1 Draw a sloped body box shape for the main part of the car. Then draw a roof box shape towards the back.

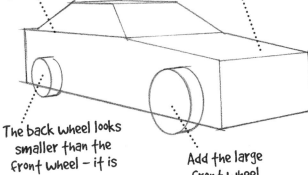

This line slopes upwards slightly

The body box shape slopes down towards the front

The back wheel looks smaller than the front wheel – it is further away

Add the large front wheel

2 Begin to shape the body of your car. Add rough shapes at the front for the lights, radiator grills and number plate.

Draw lines to create the windows

Rough shapes will form the radiator grills

Add inner ellipses to the wheels

3 Use curved lines to shape the corners of the car. Add the wing mirror and two door handles.

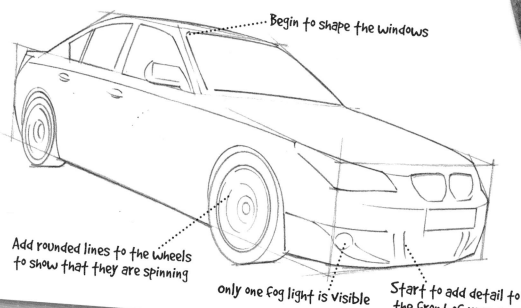

Begin to shape the windows

Add rounded lines to the wheels to show that they are spinning

only one fog light is visible

Start to add detail to the front of your car

4 Erase the guide shapes. Draw in the doors and some rough inside detail through the glass.

Draw the passenger head rest

Add a circle for the badge on the bonnet

Start to shade the paintwork to show the shape of the car

Begin to shade the wheels and radiator grills

5 Build up the dark green colour slowly. Leave the surfaces that are angled upwards lighter, as more light falls on them. Use shades of blue to colour the car's lights. You can use gentle fades and sharp edges to show reflections or details through the glass of the windscreen and lights.

The detail in the wheels is blurred because they are spinning

Porsche

1 Draw a large body box shape for the main part of the car and a roof box shape towards the back on top. Add ellipses for the two visible wheels.

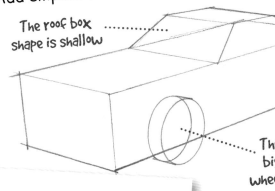

The roof box shape is shallow

Notice that the roof box shape does not reach the back

The front wheel looks bigger than the back wheel because it is closer

2 Start to make the edges rounded using short, straight lines. Draw a pointed shape for the spoiler at the back.

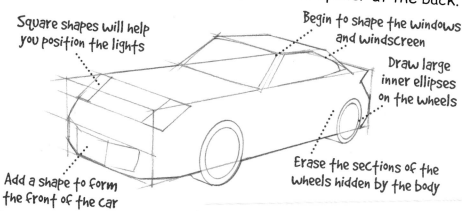

Square shapes will help you position the lights

Begin to shape the windows and windscreen

Draw large inner ellipses on the wheels

Add a shape to form the front of the car

Erase the sections of the wheels hidden by the body

3 Start to make all the corners of the car rounded by drawing smooth curves over the top of the guidelines.

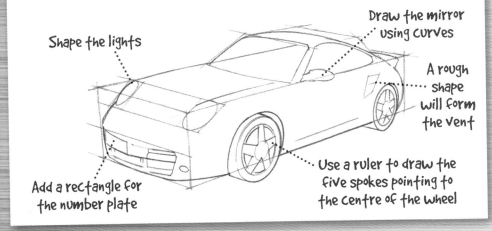

Shape the lights

Draw the mirror using curves

A rough shape will form the vent

Add a rectangle for the number plate

Use a ruler to draw the five spokes pointing to the centre of the wheel

60

4 Rub out the guide shapes. Draw in the details, making sure they are all smooth and curved.

Add lines of shaping

Draw the door handle and doors

Place the badge

A circle indicates the big brakes behind the wheels

Begin to add shading

The windows are very dark, so use a mixture of black, blue and green

5 Use shades of yellow to colour your car. Adding a little orange and green will make it look even more shiny. Leave some parts white to show where the surface of the car catches the light.

Smart car

1 Draw a sloped body box shape for the main part of the car. Add a roof box shape above it, sloping down to the front of the body box shape.

The slope at the back is short

The long slope to the front will become the windscreen

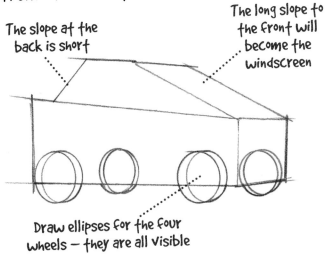

Draw ellipses for the four wheels — they are all visible

2 Start to shape the front and back of the car. Add rough shapes for the seats.

This guideline will be rubbed out because the car's roof is down

Start to shape the windscreen

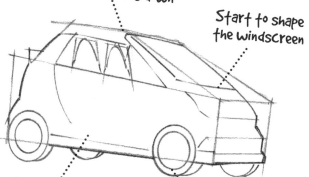

Rub out the sections of the wheels you cannot see

Add inner ellipses to the wheels on this side of the car

3 Begin to add detail to the body of the car. Draw nine thin spokes on each of the two visible wheels, all pointing to the centre.

Add the wing mirror

Draw rough shapes for the lights

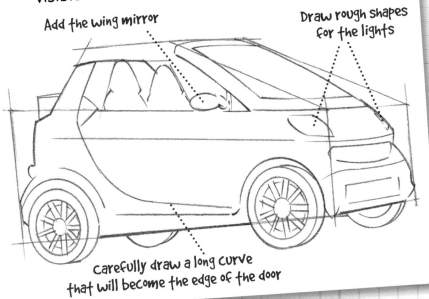

Carefully draw a long curve that will become the edge of the door

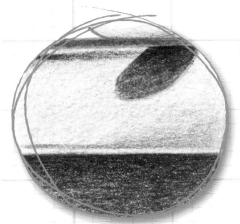

A blunt pencil will help to create a glossy paint effect. Change the level of shading where the panels bend and show shadows with dark shapes.

4 You can now rub out the guide shapes to show an open top to the car. Draw in all the small details and add shading.

Draw the petrol cap

Shape the seats

The rearview mirror can be seen through the glass

Add the back lights

Draw windscreen wipers using straight lines

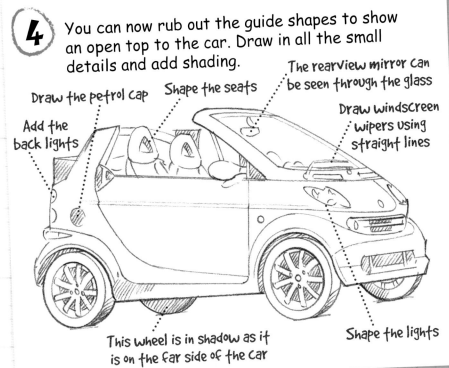

This wheel is in shadow as it is on the far side of the car

Shape the lights

5 This car has a mix of silver and purple panels. Try to build up the colour slowly and make it as even as possible. The paint shows a shadow cast by the wing mirror, so you will need to use a darker purple. Colour the lights at the back of the car red.

Shade lightly above this line, as there is a bend in the body

Lamborghini

1 Draw a large body box shape getting slightly lower for the front of the car. Then draw a low roof box shape on top.

This line will help you form the back of the car

The front of the car looks narrow, as we are viewing it from behind

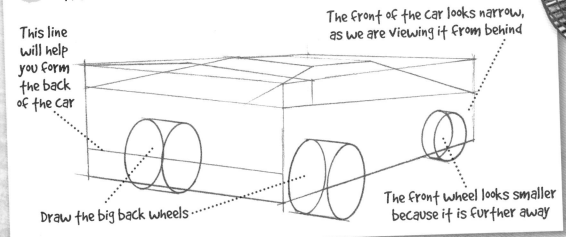

Draw the big back wheels

The front wheel looks smaller because it is further away

Use a sharp pencil for the black rubber skid marks and then use a blunt grey pencil for the smoke. To make the smoke softer, rub it with your finger.

2 Start to shape the body at the back. Add the wheel arches and shape them using straight lines.

Add the large spoiler to the back

Draw a small box shape

Use completely straight lines

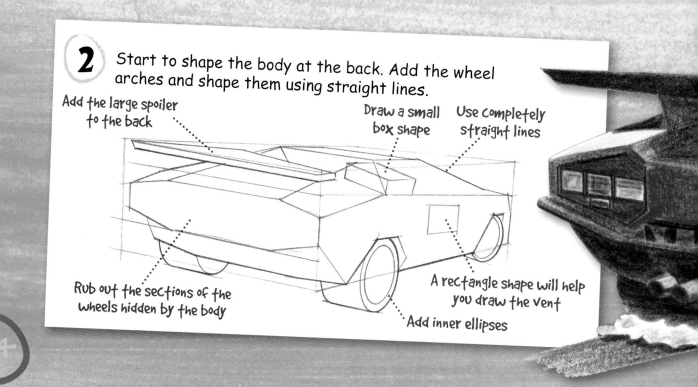

Rub out the sections of the wheels hidden by the body

A rectangle shape will help you draw the vent

Add inner ellipses

3 Continue adding the detail using straight lines. Begin to shape the small windows.

Rough shapes will help you position the area where the lights sit

Continue shaping the wheel arches

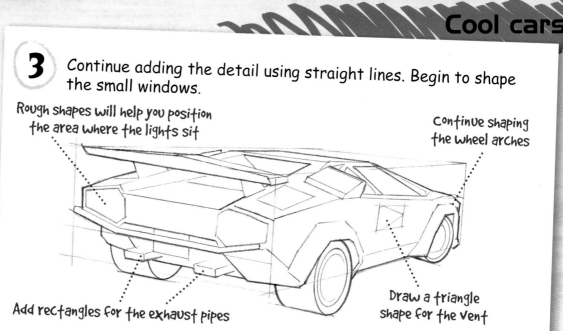

Add rectangles for the exhaust pipes

Draw a triangle shape for the vent

4 Erase the guide shapes. Draw slightly curved lines at the corners of the wheel arches and along the side of the car. Add lots of little details and shading.

Divide the windows

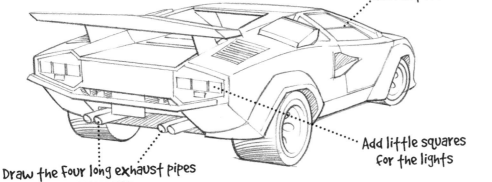

Add little squares for the lights

Draw the four long exhaust pipes

5 Colour the sides of the car with a blunt red pencil. There are lots of hard edges on the car, so the colour will change from dark on the sides to light on the top.

Clouds of white smoke and skid marks under the rear wheels show action and speed

Stock car

1 Draw a large body box shape that slopes down at the front. Add a roof box shape on top that goes right to the back of the body box shape.

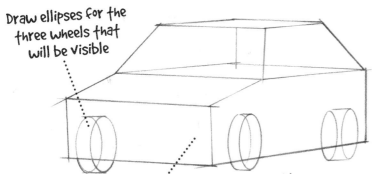

Draw ellipses for the three wheels that will be visible

The box shape is lower on this side — the car is leaning as it goes round a corner

2 Draw lines for the bumper and rectangles for the lights using a ruler. Start to draw the shape of the door.

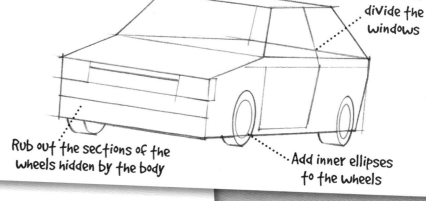

A line will divide the windows

Rub out the sections of the wheels hidden by the body

Add inner ellipses to the wheels

3 Begin to draw the windows and curved wheel arches.

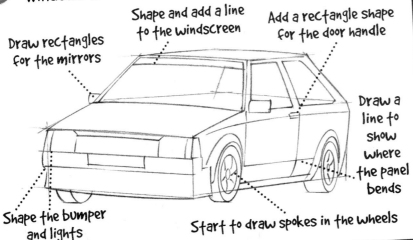

Shape and add a line to the windscreen

Add a rectangle shape for the door handle

Draw rectangles for the mirrors

Draw a line to show where the panel bends

Shape the bumper and lights

Start to draw spokes in the wheels

To show that the car is going round a sharp bend, draw a very small gap between the tyre and the wheel arch.

4 Erase the guide shapes. Add the details, such as the wipers and petrol cap. You can now add a unique pattern to the outside of your car.

Stones and dirt fly up behind the wheels

Begin to add shading

Stripes need to change direction as they bend over the corners of the body panels

5 Colour the main body of your car using a blue pencil. You can make the pattern and bumper a different colour for contrast. The glass has both dark and light areas.

Use shades of brown to colour the ground, dirt and stones

Aston Martin

1 Draw a large body box shape. Add a roof box shape with sloping sides on top.

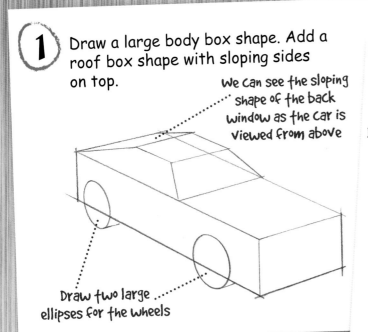

We can see the sloping shape of the back window as the car is viewed from above

Draw two large ellipses for the wheels

2 Start to shape the front and back of the body of your car. Add shapes for the lights.

Draw a rough shape to form the windows

Start to shape the windscreen with straight lines

Add inner ellipses to the wheels

3 Make all the corners of the car smooth and add extra details, such as the radiator grill, number plate and lines of shaping on the bonnet.

The wing mirrors have straight edges

Use gentle curves to make the corners smooth

The wheels have lots of small spokes, all pointing to the centre

only one fog light is visible

68

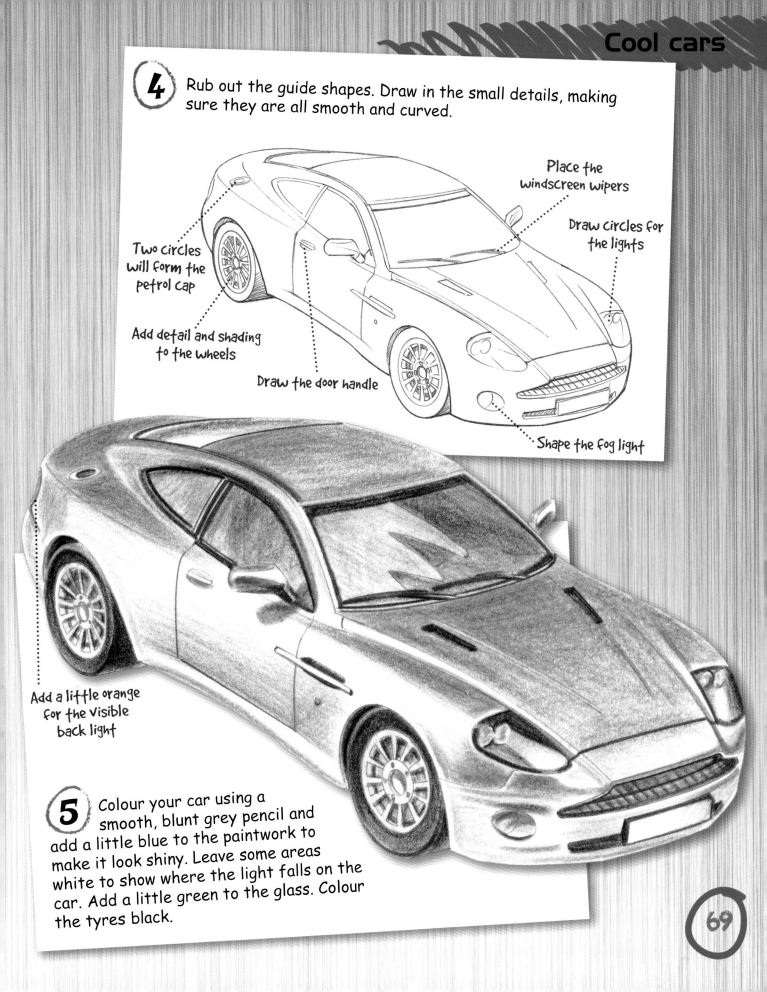

4 Rub out the guide shapes. Draw in the small details, making sure they are all smooth and curved.

Place the windscreen wipers

Draw circles for the lights

Two circles will form the petrol cap

Add detail and shading to the wheels

Draw the door handle

Shape the fog light

Add a little orange for the visible back light

5 Colour your car using a smooth, blunt grey pencil and add a little blue to the paintwork to make it look shiny. Leave some areas white to show where the light falls on the car. Add a little green to the glass. Colour the tyres black.

69

Jeep

1 Draw a big body box shape for the main part of your car. On top of this add a roof box shape at the back.

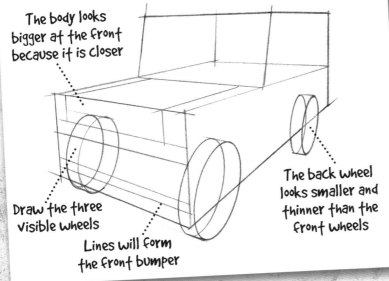

The body looks bigger at the front because it is closer

Draw the three visible wheels

Lines will form the front bumper

The back wheel looks smaller and thinner than the front wheels

Use a sharp black pencil and draw three zigzag lines to create tyre tread. Use blunt brown and black pencils to shade the tyre around the tread.

2 Shape the front of your car. Draw the wheel arches using straight lines.

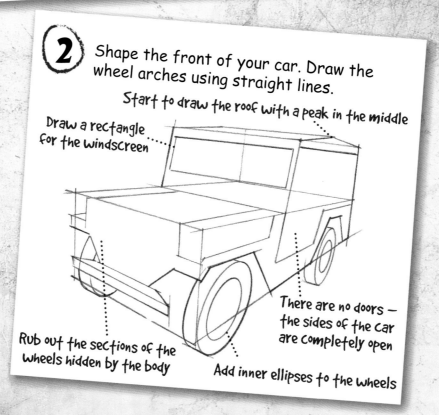

Start to draw the roof with a peak in the middle

Draw a rectangle for the windscreen

There are no doors — the sides of the car are completely open

Rub out the sections of the wheels hidden by the body

Add inner ellipses to the wheels

3 Continue to add detail with straight lines. Start to shape the seat inside.

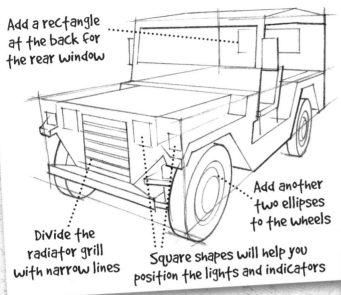

Add a rectangle at the back for the rear window

Divide the radiator grill with narrow lines

Square shapes will help you position the lights and indicators

Add another two ellipses to the wheels

4 Add the details and complete the roof, using curved lines to make it look like it is made of a soft material.

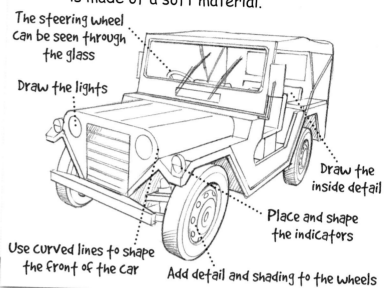

The steering wheel can be seen through the glass

Draw the lights

Use curved lines to shape the front of the car

Draw the inside detail

Place and shape the indicators

Add detail and shading to the wheels

5 Jeeps are often painted in a pattern of green colours for camouflage. Make sure the surfaces are an even colour, as the paint has no shine.

Use an orange pencil to colour the indicators

Ferrari

1 Draw a low, flat body box shape for the main part of the car. On top of this add a small, sloping shape, which will become the windscreen.

The front wheel is a different angle to the back wheel because it is turning

Add the two visible wheels

2 Draw rounded edges at the back and make the front pointed.

Begin to draw the seats

Start to shape the windscreen

Add inner ellipses to the wheels

Shape the long, thin light

Add the radiator grills

3 Start to make the corners of the car smooth and add extra details. The wheels have five thin, double spokes.

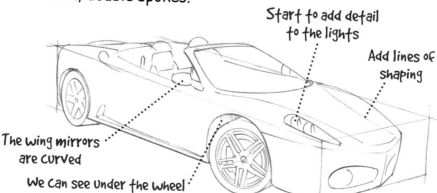

Start to add detail to the lights

Add lines of shaping

The wing mirrors are curved

We can see under the wheel arch, as the wheel is turned

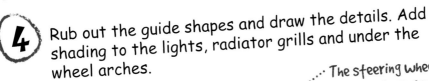

4 Rub out the guide shapes and draw the details. Add shading to the lights, radiator grills and under the wheel arches.

Shade the vent ····

···· The steering wheel and rearview mirror can be seen through the windscreen

Use shading to show the outline of the circular brake disc ·····

Adding a green tint to the glass will make the yellow seats look slightly green through it

5 Use smooth, even pencil strokes to build up the glossy red paintwork. The leather seats can be coloured in shades of yellow and light brown.

Mercedes

1 Draw a body box shape, much lower at the front than at the back. Add a roof box shape on top, towards the back.

Draw ellipses for the three wheels that will be visible

These wheels are slightly turned, so they look wider than the back wheel

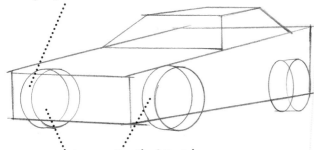

2 Draw the outlines of the doors and the door openings using straight lines.

The doors open upwards

Rub out the sections of the wheels hidden behind the body

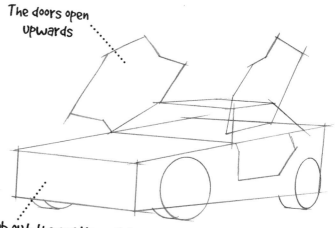

3 Begin to shape the body of your car and the doors. Draw the windows in the doors using straight lines.

Add a circular badge

Draw the radiator grill using gentle curves

Square shapes will help position the lights

Draw two ellipses on the wheels

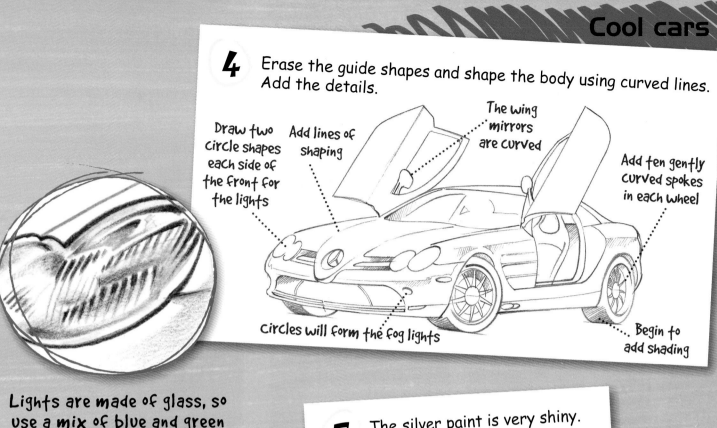

4 Erase the guide shapes and shape the body using curved lines. Add the details.

Draw two circle shapes each side of the front for the lights

Add lines of shaping

The wing mirrors are curved

Add ten gently curved spokes in each wheel

Circles will form the fog lights

Begin to add shading

Lights are made of glass, so use a **mix** of blue and green colours. Draw lines of black shading that are thick at one end and thin at the other to make it look like there are ridges in the glass.

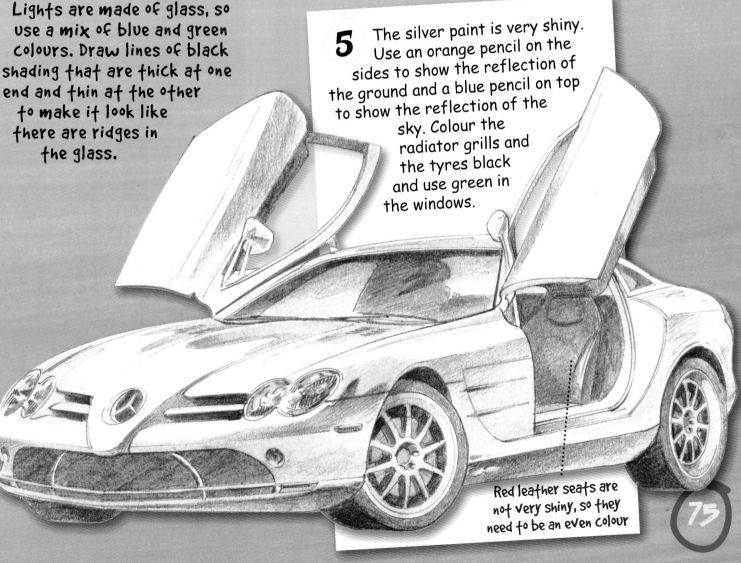

5 The silver paint is very shiny. Use an orange pencil on the sides to show the reflection of the ground and a blue pencil on top to show the reflection of the sky. Colour the radiator grills and the tyres black and use green in the windows.

Red leather seats are not very shiny, so they need to be an even colour

75

Rally car

1 Draw a sloped body box shape for the main body of the car and a roof box shape on top. Add ellipses for the four wheels, as they will all be visible.

The body box shape slopes down towards the front

This line slopes upwards

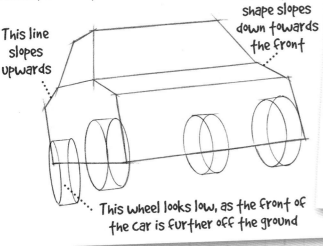

This wheel looks low, as the front of the car is further off the ground

2 Add rough shapes for the front lights and the radiator grills.

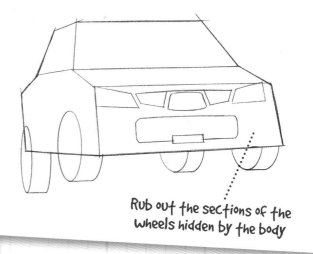

Rub out the sections of the wheels hidden by the body

3 Begin to shape the corners of the body. Add the wheel arches and inner ellipses to the wheels.

Add a shape for the windows

Make the corners rounded

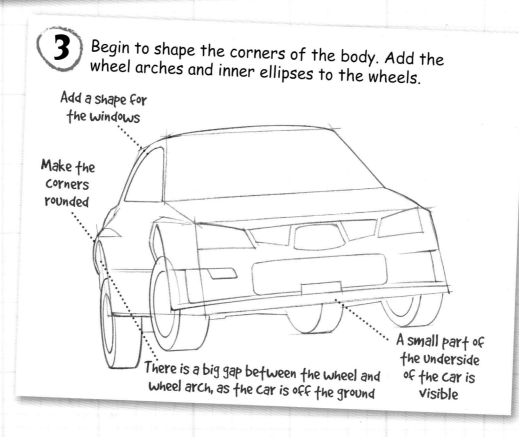

There is a big gap between the wheel and wheel arch, as the car is off the ground

A small part of the underside of the car is visible

4 Add detail to the wheels and add the final bodywork parts, such as the rear spoiler, the door handles and the wing mirrors.

Place the roof vent ·····

Draw unique graphics on your car

Begin to shade under the wheel arches

Draw the spokes and shade the wheels

Add stones and dirt flying up

Shade the radiator grills

Use sharp brown and orange pencils to draw dirt and stones flying up from the tyres. Draw little lines behind them or smudge them with your finger to make them look like they are moving.

Gold wheels can be shown with yellow and orange pencils

5 Colour your car red and leave the graphics white for contrast. The underside of the car needs to be dark. Use different shades of blue and green for the glass. Add lines of tread to the tyres.

F1 racing car

1 Draw a shallow body box shape and four huge wheels. On top of the body box shape, add a triangle shape at the back of the car.

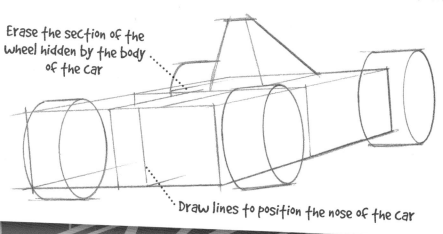

Erase the section of the wheel hidden by the body of the car

Draw lines to position the nose of the car

2 Draw the big spoilers at the front and back of the car. Add inner ellipses to the wheels.

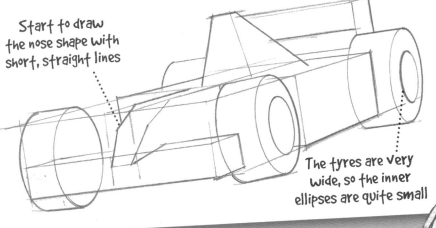

Start to draw the nose shape with short, straight lines

The tyres are very wide, so the inner ellipses are quite small

The detail in the wheels is blurred to show that they are spinning fast. Use a blunt pencil to make the edges of the shapes soft. Then use your finger to gently smudge the colour, making it even softer.

3 Begin to shape the sides of the car and the front spoiler. Add a circle in the centre for the drivers helmet.

Add the small mirrors

Create a gentle curve for the nose shape

Draw straight lines joining the body of the car to the large front wheels

4 Use curved lines to finish shaping the body. Shade the holes in the body and the wheels.

Add extra ellipses to the large wheels

Shade and add a pattern to the driver's helmet

Start to add graphics to your car

5 Colour the car green and the graphics red and white for contrast. The top surfaces should be the lightest. There is no tread on the tyres, so colour them slowly to make sure they look smooth.

Make the tops of the tyres pale, as the light is shining on them

First published in 2010 by Miles Kelly Publishing Ltd
Harding's Barn, Bardfield End Green, Thaxted, Essex, CM6 3PX, UK

Copyright © Miles Kelly Publishing Ltd 2010

This edition published 2013

2 4 6 8 10 9 7 5 3 1

PUBLISHING DIRECTOR Belinda Gallagher
CREATIVE DIRECTOR Jo Cowan
EDITORS Carly Blake, Rosie McGuire, Sarah Parkin
DESIGNERS Jo Cowan, Michelle Canntella,
Candice Bekir, Kayleigh Allen
COVER DESIGN Rob Hale
PRODUCTION MANAGER Elizabeth Collins
REPROGRAPHICS Stephan Davis,
Jennifer Hunt, Thom Allaway
ASSETS Lorraine King

ISBN 978-1-78209-101-1

Printed in China

British Library Cataloguing-in-Publication Data
A catalogue record for this book is available from the British Library

ACKNOWLEDGEMENTS
The publishers would like to thank the following sources
for the use of their photographs:
Shutterstock.com Cover (front) Nattika (coloured pencils), (back) Picsfive (pencil),
lenetstan (coloured pencils)
Page 4 nomad/Fotolia.com; 50–51 da-kuk/iStockphoto.com; 52–53 Kirsty Pargeter/Fotolia.com;
62-63 Sharpshot/Fotolia.com; 70–71 Lizard/Fotolia.com

All other images are from the Miles Kelly Archives

www.mileskelly.net
info@mileskelly.net

www.factsforprojects.com